A Beginning-to-Read Book

A Visit to the Aquarium

by Mary Lindeen

Norwood House Press

DEAR CAREGIVER, The *Beginning to Read—Read and Discover* books provide emergent readers the opportunity to explore the world through nonfiction while building early reading skills. The text integrates both common sight words and content vocabulary. These key words are featured on lists provided at the back of the book to help your child expand his or her sight word recognition, which helps build reading fluency. The content words expand vocabulary and support comprehension.

Nonfiction text is any text that is factual. The Common Core State Standards call for an increase in the amount of informational text reading among students. The Standards aim to promote college and career readiness among students. Preparation for college and career endeavors requires proficiency in reading complex informational texts in a variety of content areas. You can help your child build a foundation by introducing nonfiction early. To further support the CCSS, you will find Reading Reinforcement activities at the back of the book that are aligned to these Standards.

Above all, the most important part of the reading experience is to have fun and enjoy it!

Sincerely,

Shannon Cannon

Shannon Cannon, Ph.D.
Literacy Consultant

Norwood House Press • P.O. Box 316598 • Chicago, Illinois 60631
For more information about Norwood House Press please visit our website at
www.norwoodhousepress.com or call 866-565-2900.

Editor: Judy Kentor Schmauss

Designer: Lindaanne Donohoe

Photo Credits:

Phil Martin, cover, 10-11; Shutterstock, 1, 3, 4-5, 6, 7, 8-9, 18-19, 20-21, 26-27, 28-29; Dreamstime, 12-13 (©Songnick), 22-23 (©Marco Jimenez), 24 (Noblige); iStock, 14-15, 16-17, 25

Library of Congress Cataloging-in-Publication Data

Lindeen, Mary, author.
A visit to the aquarium / by Mary Lindeen.
pages cm. – (A beginning to read book)
Summary: "Take a trip to the local aquarium. See the fish, turtles, sharks, and other sea animals that live there. Learn about the dolphin trainer and veterinarian who work there. This title includes reading activities and a word list"– Provided by publisher.
Audience: K to grade 3
ISBN 978-1-59953-694-1 (library edition : alk. paper)
ISBN 978-1-60357-779-3 (ebook)
1. Public aquariums–Juvenile literature. 2. Public aquariums–Employees–Juvenile literature. I. Title.
QL78.L56 2015
597.073–dc23

2014047634

Manufactured in the United States of America in Stevens Point, Wisconsin. 275N–062015

Fish can live in many places.
They can live in the sea.
They can live in a pond.
They can live in a bowl.

This place is home to many fish.

It is an aquarium.

Look at this big fish tank!
How many fish do you see?

What do you see in this tank?

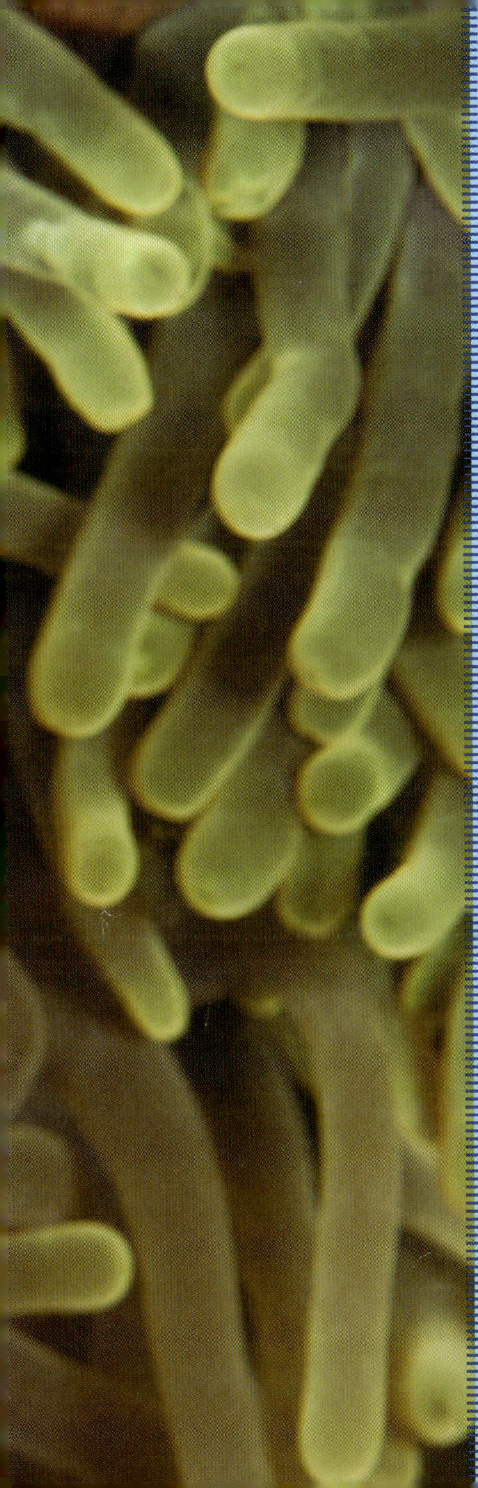

These fish are clown fish.

How do they look like clowns?

These fish are catfish.

How do they look like cats?

Other water animals live here, too.

These turtles are sea turtles.

Their flippers help them swim.

This octopus lives in the aquarium.

Seahorses live here, too.

Look how little they are!

This shark lives in the aquarium.

It lives in a big tank.

These dolphins put on a show.

Trainers teach them how to do tricks.

This fish is sick.

The veterinarian will make it well.

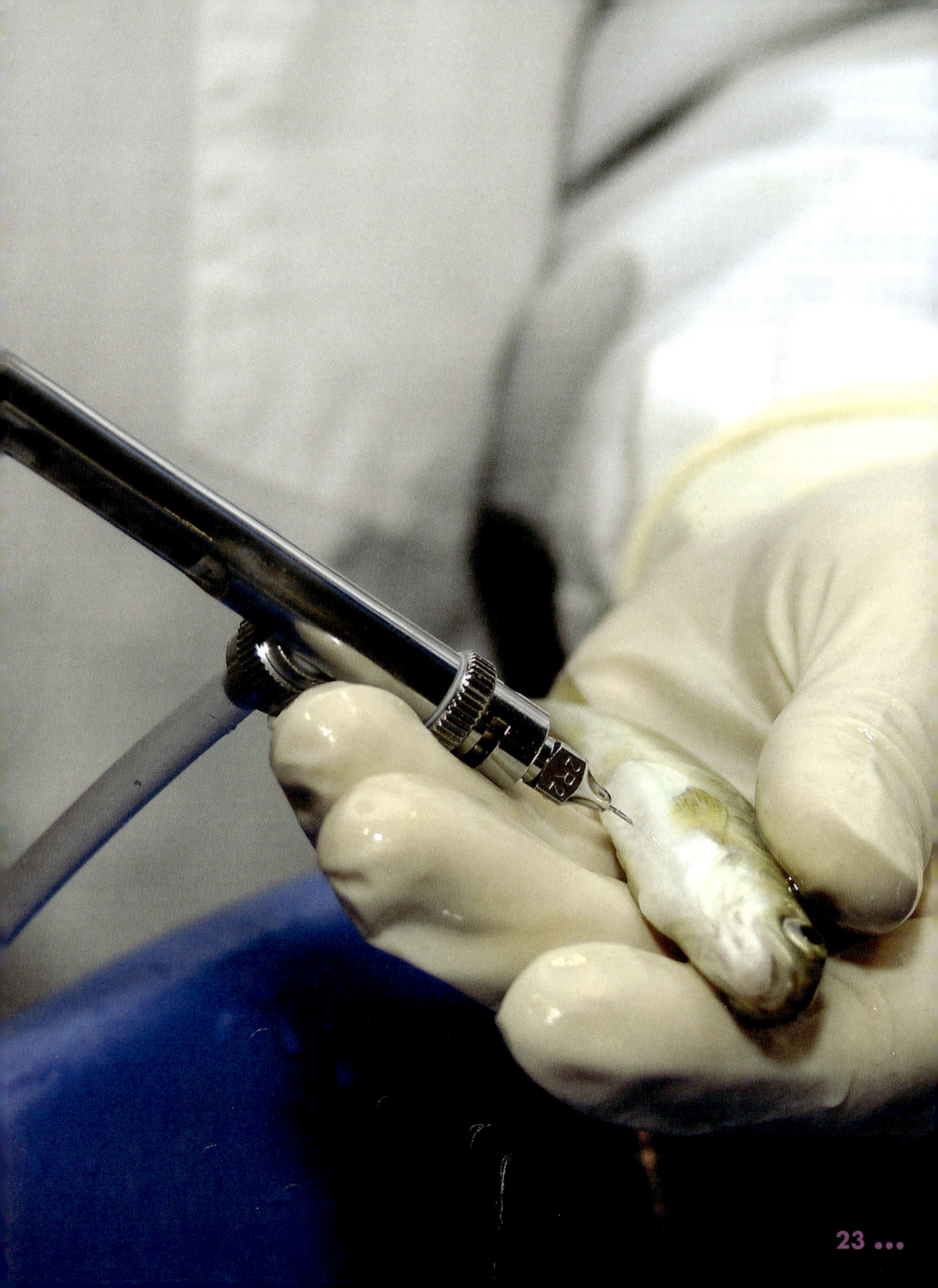

Look at the starfish
in this tide pool.

You can hold a starfish
if you want to!

This aquarium has penguins.

They swim in the water.

You can see so many animals at the aquarium.

Which one would you like to see?

. . . READING REINFORCEMENT . . .

CRAFT AND STRUCTURE

To check your child's understanding of this book, recreate the following diagram on a sheet of paper. Read the book with your child, and then help him or her fill in the diagram using what they learned. Work together and use this book to identify animals that live in an aquarium and people who work there.

Animals at the Aquarium	Workers at the Aquarium

VOCABULARY: Learning Content Words

Content words are words that are specific to a particular topic. All of the content words for this book can be found on page 32. Use some or all of these content words to complete one or more of the following activities:

- Create an idea web for the content words. Write a content word in the middle of the diagram. Help your child write related words and ideas in the outer circles.
- Write each word and each definition on separate cards. Play a memory game by turning all cards face down and then turning them over to find matching pairs of words and definitions.
- Have your child find and cut out two magazine pictures that remind him or her of the meaning of each content word.
- Make up a story together using as many of the content words as you can.
- Ask your child questions that include one or more of the content words. Each question should begin with one of these words: *who, what, when, where, why,* or *how*.

FOUNDATIONAL SKILLS: Multisyllabic words

Multisyllabic words are words with more than one syllable. Have your child identify the number of syllables in each of the words below. Then ask your child to find multisyllabic words in this book.

aquarium	turtles	catfish
flippers	whale	veterinarian
seahorses	animals	tricks

CLOSE READING OF INFORMATIONAL TEXT

Close reading helps children comprehend text. It includes reading a text, discussing it with others, and answering questions about it. Use these questions to discuss this book with your child:

- What is an aquarium?
- What does a veterinarian do?
- What is one animal that lives in a tide pool?
- Which part of a sea turtle helps it move through the water?
- How is an aquarium like a zoo? How is it different?
- Why do people visit an aquarium?

FLUENCY

Fluency is the ability to read accurately with speed and expression. Help your child practice fluency by using one or more of the following activities:

- Reread this book to your child at least two times while he or she uses a finger to track each word as you read it.
- Read the first sentence aloud. Then have your child reread the sentence with you. Continue until you have finished this book.
- Ask your child to read aloud the words they know on each page of this book. (Your child will learn additional words with subsequent readings.)
- Have your child practice reading this book several times to improve accuracy, rate, and expression.

••• Word List •••

A Visit to the Aquarium uses the 71 words listed below. *High-frequency* words are those words tha are used most often in the English language. They are sometimes referred to as sight words because children need to learn to recognize them automatically when they read. *Content words* are any words specific to a particular topic. Regular practice reading these words will enhance your child's ability to read with greater fluency and comprehension.

High-Frequency Words

a	here	look	show	too
an	home	make	so	want
are	how	many	the	water
at	if	on	their	well
big	in	one	them	what
can	is	other	these	which
do	it	place(s)	they	will
has	like	put	this	would
help	little	see	to	you

Content Words

animals	fish	pool	swim	turtles
aquarium	flippers	sea	tank	veterinaria
catfish	hold	seahorses	teach	
cats	live(s)	shark	tide	
clown(s)	octopus	sick	trainers	
dolphins	penguins	starfish	tricks	

••• About the Author

Mary Lindeen is a writer, editor, parent, and former elementary school teacher. She has written more than 100 books for children and edited many more. She specializes in early literacy instruction and books for young readers, especially nonfiction.

••• About the Advisor

Dr. Shannon Cannon is a teacher educator in the School of Education at UC Davis, where she also earned her Ph.D. in Language, Literacy, and Culture. She serves on the clinical faculty, supervising pre-service teachers and teaching elementary methods courses in reading, effective teaching, and teacher action research.